The Art of Effective Leadership

Practical Strategies

By: Ahmed Alhafidh

The Art of Effective Leadership

Practical Strategies

Copyright © 2024 by Ahmed Alhafidh

All rights reserved.

No part of this book may be reproduced, stored in a retrieval system, or transmitted in any form or by any means, electronic, mechanical, photo-copying, recording, or otherwise, without the prior written permission of the author, except for brief quotations in critical reviews or articles.

To all the people I love.

Preface

In a world that is continuously evolving, the demand for effective leadership has never been more crucial. Whether in the boardroom or the classroom, on the sports field or within non-profit organizations, leadership manifests itself in myriad forms. Yet at its core, successful leadership is about influencing others, fostering collaboration, and driving positive change. The perspectives and strategies outlined in this book seek to illuminate the multiplicity of leadership styles that exist across various fields, showcasing that while contexts may differ, fundamental principles remain constant.

The concept of leadership is an intricate tapestry woven from experiences, traits, principles, and methodologies unique to every domain. From business and education to healthcare and social justice, each chapter in this book presents the essential qualities and practices necessary for effective leadership within that specific context. The aim is to provide a comprehensive guide that not only recognizes the uniqueness of each field but also underscores the shared attributes of great leaders.

As you embark on this journey through "The Art of Effective Leadership" you will encounter stories of visionary leaders, innovative strategies, and actionable insights that can be integrated into your own leadership approach. The content is rooted in research and enriched by real-world examples, ensuring relevance across diverse audiences, whether you are an aspiring leader, an experienced executive, or someone passionately engaged in your community.

We live in times of rapid change—technological advancements, social movements, and global challenges demand that we adapt our leadership styles and strategies accordingly. This book addresses that need, highlighting the importance of emotional intelligence, adaptability, and resilience, which are essential traits for leaders in any field. The hope is that you will find inspiration within these pages to not only enhance your own leadership capabilities but also to inspire and uplift others in your journey.

Moreover, each chapter serves as a standalone resource, allowing readers to delve into areas of interest or relevance. Whether you seek to lead in a corporate setting, within a creative arts community, or in the pursuit of social justice, this book provides valuable insights tailored to your leadership aspirations.

As you turn the pages, keep in mind that leadership is not a destination but a constant journey of growth and learning. Embrace the knowledge shared here, reflect on your experiences, and actively seek opportunities to apply what resonates with you.

Thank you for joining me on this exploration of effective leadership across diverse fields. My hope is that "**The Art of Effective Leadership**" equips you with the tools and inspiration you need to navigate your leadership journey successfully, fostering a positive impact in every aspect of your life, and the lives of those around you.

Let's begin this journey together.

Ahmed Alhafidh

Contents

Chapter 1: Leadership in Business............................ 1

Chapter 2: Leadership in Education....................... 10

Chapter 3: Leadership in Non-Profit Organizations
.... 20

Chapter 4: Leadership in Sports............................. 30

Chapter 5: Leadership in Healthcare 39

Chapter 6: Leadership in Technology...................... 50

Chapter 7: Leadership in Government 61

Chapter 8: Leadership in the Arts 71

Chapter 9: Leadership in Social Justice 81

Chapter 10: Leadership in Environmentalism....... 92

Chapter 11: Leadership in Family Dynamics....... 103

Chapter 12: Leadership in Personal Growth........ 113

Chapter 1: Leadership in Business

Introduction

In the ever-evolving landscape of the business world, effective leadership is not merely an advantage; it is a necessity. Leaders wield considerable influence over their organizations, impacting not just financial performance, but also company culture, employee satisfaction, customer loyalty, and sustainability. As businesses navigate the complexities of globalization, technological advancements, and shifting consumer expectations, the qualities that define successful leaders continue to evolve. This chapter delves into the fundamental aspects of effective leadership in business, equipping aspiring leaders with the tools they need to thrive in a competitive environment.

The Visionary Leader

Cultivating a Clear Vision

At the heart of effective business leadership lies a compelling vision. A successful leader articulates a clear and inspiring vision that directs the organization's strategy and operations. This vision serves as a beacon, guiding employees toward common goals and motivating them to invest their efforts in collective success.

Take, for example, the leadership of Elon Musk at Tesla and SpaceX. Musk's vision extends beyond simply selling electric cars or launching rockets; it encompasses a broader ambition to accelerate the world's transition to sustainable energy and ensure the survival of humanity by becoming a multi-planetary species. By clearly communicating this vision, Musk inspires his teams to work tirelessly toward these ambitious goals, even in the face of significant challenges.

Components of a Compelling Vision

Creating a compelling vision involves understanding the core values and purpose of the organization. Leaders must engage in a thorough analysis of both external market dynamics and internal capabilities. A well-defined vision includes:

1. **Purpose**: What is the organization's reason for existence beyond profit-making? A purpose-driven vision resonates deeply and connects with employees' values.

2. **Direction**: The vision must clearly outline the organization's long-term aspirations and the trajectory towards achieving those goals.

3. **Inspirational Element**: A vision should be aspirational and ambitious, sparking excitement and enthusiasm among stakeholders.

4. **Flexibility**: While a vision must be steadfast, it should also be adaptable to changing circumstances in the business environment.

Communicating the Vision

Once a vision is established, communicating it effectively across all levels of the organization is vital. A leader must use various mediums—town hall meetings, internal communications, and social media—to share the vision in a manner that resonates with employees.

Leaders can amplify their communication by incorporating storytelling techniques that illustrate the vision's impact on people's lives. This not only helps employees understand their role in fulfilling the vision but also cultivates a sense of ownership and belonging.

Communication: The Keystone of Leadership

Importance of Effective Communication

Effective communication is often cited as the most critical skill of successful leaders. It involves not only conveying information but also listening actively and fostering open dialogue. Strong communicators can inspire teams, build trust, and navigate challenging situations.

The Elements of Effective Communication

1. **Clarity**: Leaders must communicate with clarity to avoid misunderstandings. Clear messaging helps ensure that all team members are on the same page regarding expectations, goals, and strategies.

2. **Empathy**: Beyond clarity, understanding the emotions and perspectives of team members is essential. Empathetic communication fosters deeper connections, enabling leaders to address concerns and build trust.

3. **Feedback**: Strong leaders encourage feedback to cultivate a culture of continuous improvement. Actively seeking input demonstrates a willingness to listen and adapt, ultimately strengthening team dynamics.

4. **Consistency**: Consistency in messaging reinforces credibility. Leaders must ensure that their words align with actions to maintain trust amongst their teams.

Techniques for Effective Communication

1. **Active Listening**: Leaders should practice active listening by fully engaging in conversations and reflecting back the key points. This demonstrates respect and encourages open dialogue.

2. **Regular Check-Ins**: Implementing regular one-on-one check-ins with team members provides opportunities for ongoing communication and relationship building.

3. **Utilizing Technology**: Leveraging communication platforms—such as Slack, Microsoft Teams, or video conferencing—can facilitate timely updates and inclusive discussions.

4. **Storytelling**: Engaging storytelling captures attention and creates emotional connections. Leaders can use stories to articulate their vision and convey values compellingly.

Adaptability and Resilience

The Need for Flexibility

The business landscape is characterized by rapid change, which can present both challenges and opportunities. Effective leaders must exhibit adaptability and resilience to navigate these dynamics successfully.

Building a Culture of Adaptability

1. **Encouraging Innovation**: Fostering a culture of innovation encourages team members to think creatively and embrace change. Leaders can support experimentation and reward calculated risks to stimulate growth.

2. **Continuous Learning**: Leaders should cultivate a mindset of continuous learning, both for themselves and their employees. Investing in professional development through training and resources prepares the team to cope with new challenges.

3. **Emphasizing Collaboration**: Promoting collaboration within teams enables diverse perspectives to converge, yielding innovative solutions to problems.

Resilience in Leadership

1. **Leading by Example**: Resilience is infectious. Leaders who model perseverance through adversity inspire their teams to adopt a similar mindset.

2. **Crisis Management**: Effective leaders anticipate potential crises and develop contingency plans. By proactively addressing challenges, leaders can instill confidence and mitigate disruptions.

3. **Promoting Well-Being**: Encouraging a healthy work-life balance and supporting employees' mental well-being helps build resilience within the organization.

Emotional Intelligence in Business Leadership

The Essence of Emotional Intelligence

Emotional intelligence (EI) encompasses the ability to recognize, understand, and manage one's emotions, as well as the emotions of others. In the business context, leaders with high emotional intelligence can foster stronger relationships, enhance team collaboration, and drive performance.

Components of Emotional Intelligence

1. **Self-Awareness**: Leaders must recognize their strengths and weaknesses. Self-aware leaders can better manage their emotions and reactions, allowing them to respond to situations thoughtfully.

2. **Self-Regulation**: The ability to control impulsive feelings and behaviors is crucial for

maintaining professionalism. Leaders who practice self-regulation can stay composed in high-pressure situations.

3. **Empathy**: Understanding the emotional state of team members allows leaders to provide support and guidance, thereby enhancing team cohesion and morale.

4. **Social Skills**: Leaders need strong interpersonal skills to inspire and influence others effectively. Building rapport, fostering collaboration, and resolving conflicts are crucial aspects of social skills.

5. **Motivation**: Emotionally intelligent leaders are self-motivated and align their goals with those of their teams, encouraging a sense of shared purpose.

Enhancing Emotional Intelligence

1. **Practicing Mindfulness**: Mindfulness practices, such as meditation, promote self-awareness and emotional regulation, allowing leaders to reduce stress and maintain focus.

2. **Soliciting Feedback**: Seeking feedback regarding one's leadership style provides insights into how others perceive emotions and behaviors, paving the way for personal growth.

3. **Cultivating Empathy**: Actively engaging with team members and understanding their perspectives fosters empathy, creating a healthy team environment.

Conclusion

Strong leadership is the foundation of effective business management. Visionary leadership inspires individuals to strive for excellence. Effective communication ensures clarity and fosters a culture of trust. Adaptability and resilience equip leaders to navigate an ever-changing landscape, while emotional intelligence enhances interpersonal dynamics within teams.

By embracing these tenets, aspiring leaders can cultivate a robust set of skills that will serve them well in their pursuit of impactful leadership. As the business environment continues to evolve, the importance of effective leadership only grows stronger, making the development of these characteristics essential for both personal growth and organizational success. In the chapters ahead, we will explore how these leadership qualities manifest across various fields, offering insights and strategies to empower you on your unique leadership journey.

Chapter 2: Leadership in Education

Introduction

Education is the bedrock of society, shaping the minds and futures of generations. As the landscape of education evolves—marked by technological advancements, diverse student populations, and an ever-expanding understanding of pedagogy—the role of effective leadership in educational institutions becomes increasingly critical. Leaders in education not only influence the immediate academic environment but also have the potential to effect systemic change within their communities. This chapter explores the unique dimensions of educational leadership, focusing on the qualities and strategies that are essential for fostering a thriving educational atmosphere.

The Visionary Educator

Establishing a Clear Educational Vision

Educational leaders play a pivotal role in shaping the vision for their institutions. A clear and compelling educational vision articulates the values, goals, and aspirations of the school community and serves as a guiding framework for decision-making.

For instance, consider the leadership of Dr. John Deasy during his tenure as Superintendent of Schools in Los Angeles. Deasy championed a bold vision centered around equity, access, and innovation, aiming to transform underperforming schools into hubs of excellence. By uniting stakeholders around a shared vision, he empowered educators and students alike, resulting in significant improvements in student performance.

Components of a Strong Educational Vision

An effective educational vision includes several key elements:

1. **Inclusivity**: A vision must embrace and reflect the diversity of the student body, ensuring that all voices are heard and represented.

2. **Academic Excellence**: The vision should emphasize a commitment to high academic standards and continuous improvement in teaching and learning.

3. **Community Engagement**: Engaging parents, community leaders, and local organizations is essential for a comprehensive

educational vision that fosters collaboration and support.

4. **Innovation**: Encouraging creativity and innovation in teaching practices and curriculum development can catalyze positive educational change.

Communicating the Vision Effectively

Communicating the educational vision effectively is a vital aspect of leadership in education. Leaders should use various channels to articulate their vision, ensuring it reaches teachers, students, and families. Methods for effective communication include:

1. **Regular Meetings**: Town halls and faculty meetings provide opportunities for leaders to share updates and progress regarding the vision.

2. **Visual Displays**: Creating visual representations of the vision, such as banners or infographics, can reinforce the message within the school environment.

3. **Storytelling**: Sharing success stories that highlight the impact of the vision can motivate and inspire stakeholders to embrace the shared goals.

4. **Digital Platforms**: Utilizing social media and school websites to disseminate information about the vision can help engage a broader audience.

Collaboration and Empowerment

Fostering Collaborative Leadership

In educational settings, collaborative leadership is vital for creating a culture of shared responsibility and engagement. Effective leaders prioritize collaboration among faculty, staff, and stakeholders, recognizing that diverse perspectives contribute to richer decision-making.

Building Collaborative Structures

Leaders can foster collaboration through various strategies:

1. **Professional Learning Communities (PLCs)**: Establishing PLCs encourages teachers to collaborate, share best practices, and engage in continuous professional development.

2. **Shared Leadership Models**: Distributing leadership roles across the school can empower educators to take ownership of initiatives, fostering a sense of agency and investment in the school's vision.

3. **Mentorship Programs**: Pairing experienced educators with novice teachers creates opportunities for knowledge sharing, support, and professional growth.

4. **Interdepartmental Communication**: Encouraging open lines of communication between different departments helps break down silos and fosters a sense of unity within the school.

Empowering Teachers and Staff

Effective educational leaders empower their staff by creating an environment that values input and encourages risk-taking. Empowered educators are more likely to innovate in their teaching practices, leading to enhanced student outcomes.

1. **Professional Development**: Providing access to robust professional learning opportunities supports teacher growth and enhances instructional strategies.

2. **Autonomy in Decision-Making**: Allowing teachers the autonomy to make decisions regarding their classrooms fosters a sense of trust and ownership.

3. **Recognition and Celebration**: Celebrating the accomplishments of educators creates a

positive culture that reinforces the collective effort toward the school's goals.

Building Relationships and Trust

The Role of Relationships in Education

Positive relationships are foundational to effective educational leadership. Strong relationships among educators, students, and families foster a sense of community and belonging that is essential for a thriving learning environment.

Cultivating Trust and Respect

Leaders can cultivate trust and respect through the following practices:

1. **Active Listening**: Engaging in active listening demonstrates respect for diverse perspectives and encourages open dialogue.

2. **Visibility and Accessibility**: Being present in the school community through regular interactions with teachers and students builds rapport and trust.

3. **Transparency**: Clear communication regarding decisions, changes, and challenges fosters a culture of trust and reinforces leaders' integrity.

4. **Supportive Environment**: Establishing a supportive environment in which educators and students feel safe to express their thoughts and concerns encourages meaningful connections.

Building Strong Family and Community Partnerships

Engaging families and the broader community in educational efforts is crucial for creating a strong support network. Educational leaders should prioritize building partnerships through:

1. **Open House Events**: Hosting events that invite families to engage with teachers and learn about school initiatives helps cultivate a sense of community.

2. **Regular Communication**: Communicating consistently with families through newsletters, social media, and parent-teacher conferences keeps them informed and involved.

3. **Community Engagement Projects**: Involving students and families in community service projects fosters a sense of purpose and connection to the local community.

Embracing Change and Innovation

Navigating Educational Change

Change is a constant in education, driven by advances in technology, shifts in societal needs, and evolving pedagogical frameworks. Successful leaders embrace change as an opportunity for growth and improvement.

Leading Change Initiatives

1. **Identifying Needs**: Assessing the needs of the school community can help leaders prioritize change initiatives that genuinely benefit students and educators.

2. **Stakeholder Involvement**: Engaging stakeholders in the change process fosters buy-in and collaboration, increasing the likelihood of successful implementation.

3. **Providing Resources**: Allocating the necessary resources—time, funding, and training—ensures that change initiatives are sustainable and effective.

4. **Evaluating Impact**: Continuous evaluation of implemented changes helps leaders assess their effectiveness and make data-informed adjustments.

Fostering a Culture of Innovation

Leaders can create a culture of innovation by:

1. **Encouraging Experimentation**: Providing educators with the freedom to experiment with new teaching methods encourages creative problem-solving.

2. **Recognizing Risk-Taking**: Celebrating innovative approaches, even those that may not yield immediate success, fosters a growth mindset within the school community.

3. **Embracing Technology**: Leaders should explore and integrate emerging technologies that enhance teaching and learning, preparing students for the demands of the 21st century.

Conclusion

Leadership in education requires a unique blend of vision, collaboration, relationship-building, adaptability, and innovation. Visionary educational leaders are instrumental in setting the direction for their institutions, while collaborative practices empower educators and foster a supportive community. Building strong relationships is integral to creating an inclusive and trusting environment, and embracing change is essential for sustained growth and improvement.

As we continue to explore various leadership contexts in the upcoming chapters, it is vital to recognize that the principles of effective leadership are often interwoven. The insights shared in this chapter not only serve as guiding principles for educational leaders but also contribute to the broader understanding of effective leadership in diverse fields. The educational landscape may be complex, but with the right leadership practices, it can be transformed into an environment that nurtures students and empowers educators to achieve their fullest potential.

Chapter 3: Leadership in Non-Profit Organizations

Introduction

Non-profit organizations (NPOs) play a critical role in addressing social issues, promoting civic engagement, and supporting community development. With missions that often center around humanitarian, educational, cultural, or environmental causes, non-profits require effective leadership to navigate challenges and maximize impact. As the landscape of the non-profit sector evolves—driven by funding constraints, shifting social dynamics, and technological advancements—the role of strong, adaptive leaders has never been more vital. This chapter examines the unique aspects of leadership in non-profit organizations, focusing on the essential qualities, challenges, and strategies that enable non-profit leaders to fulfill their missions and drive meaningful change.

The Purpose-Driven Leader

Establishing a Compelling Mission

At the heart of every non-profit organization is a clear and compelling mission that drives its activities and inspires its stakeholders. Non-profit leaders must clearly articulate this mission, ensuring that it resonates with both internal staff and external supporters.

For instance, consider the leadership of Melinda Gates at the Bill & Melinda Gates Foundation. Under her guidance, the foundation has focused on tackling significant global challenges such as poverty and healthcare inequity. By consistently communicating the foundation's mission and vision, she has galvanized supporters, partners, and staff toward a shared purpose.

Components of a compelling mission

An effective mission statement for a non-profit organization should include:

1. **Clarity**: The mission should be straightforward and easily understood by various stakeholders, including donors, volunteers, beneficiaries, and community members.

2. **Specificity**: A precise mission helps delineate the organization's focus areas and target populations, ensuring that efforts are directed effectively.

3. **Inspiration**: A compelling mission motivates individuals to contribute their time, talent, and resources, fostering ongoing engagement and loyalty.

4. **Demonstrable Impact**: The mission should imply a vision of measurable outcomes, reinforcing the organization's commitment to accountability and effectiveness.

Communicating the Mission Effectively

Leaders in non-profit organizations must prioritize effective communication of their mission to inspire stakeholders and motivate action.

1. **Storytelling**: Invoking powerful narratives that highlight personal experiences and successes can make the mission relatable, fostering deeper connections with supporters.

2. **Multi-Channel Outreach**: Employing various communication channels, including social media, newsletters, and public events, ensures that the mission reaches a wide audience.

3. **Visual Representation**: Infographics, videos, and other visual materials can convey complex ideas in an engaging manner that captures attention and interest.

4. **Consistency**: Recurring themes and messages across all communications create a cohesive narrative that strengthens the organization's identity in the minds of stakeholders.

Building a Community of Support

Fostering Relationships and Collaboration

A successful non-profit leader recognizes that building and nurturing relationships with stakeholders is essential for achieving impact. Non-profit organizations rely heavily on collaborations—whether with volunteers, community members, donors, or other organizations—to implement their programs effectively.

Strategies for Engaging Stakeholders

1. **Actively Involve Volunteers**: Non-profit leaders should create an inclusive environment where volunteers feel valued and engaged. Empowering volunteers through meaningful roles fosters commitment and makes them advocates for the organization.

2. **Building Donor Relationships**: Cultivating strong relationships with donors is crucial for ensuring financial sustainability. Regular updates on impact and recognition of donor contributions reinforce commitment and encourage ongoing support.

3. **Community Partnerships**: Collaborating with other organizations, local businesses, and government entities enhances resource-sharing and amplifies impact. Leaders can leverage these partnerships to reach broader audiences and achieve common objectives.

4. **Engaging Beneficiaries**: Actively involving beneficiaries in the decision-making process is essential for understanding their needs and ensuring that programs are responsive and effective.

Creating a Culture of Inclusion

Non-profit leaders can foster a culture of inclusion by:

1. **Promoting Diversity**: Actively seeking diverse perspectives and experiences enhances organizational creativity and decision-making.

2. **Encouraging Feedback**: Creating mechanisms for stakeholders to provide

feedback demonstrates a commitment to improvement and responsiveness.

3. **Empowering Staff**: Encouraging staff to take ownership of their roles and participate in strategic planning elevates engagement and innovation within the organization.

Navigating Financial Challenges

The Unique Financial Landscape of Non-Profits

Non-profit organizations often operate under financial constraints, making effective financial leadership a critical skill. Leaders must balance mission-driven activities with sustainable funding models to ensure organizational viability.

Strategies for Financial Sustainability

1. **Diverse Funding Sources**: Leaders should pursue varied revenue streams, including individual donor contributions, grants, corporate partnerships, and earned income projects, to reduce dependency on a single source of funding.

2. **Grants and Philanthropy**: Writing compelling grant proposals and fostering relationships with foundations are essential for securing funding. Non-profit leaders must

be adept at identifying funding opportunities that align with their mission.

3. **Transparency and Accountability**: Demonstrating financial transparency builds trust with donors and stakeholders. Regularly sharing financial reports and outcomes reinforces the organization's commitment to stewardship.

4. **Budgeting for Impact**: Prioritizing budget allocations based on programmatic impact ensures that resources are allocated effectively, advancing core mission goals.

Leading Through Change and Uncertainty

The Dynamic Nature of the Non-Profit Sector

The non-profit sector is often subject to changes in funding, policy, and social conditions. Effective leaders must be agile and resilient, ready to adapt their strategies in response to new challenges and opportunities.

Strategies for Effective Change Management

1. **Establishing Clear Objectives**: Clearly defined objectives provide direction during times of change, ensuring that stakeholders remain aligned with organizational goals.

2. **Open Communication**: Communicating transparently about changes and their implications fosters trust and prepares stakeholders for new directions.

3. **Embracing Flexibility**: Non-profit leaders should cultivate a culture of adaptability, encouraging staff to embrace new ideas and processes.

4. **Monitoring and Evaluation**: Regularly assessing programs and initiatives enables leaders to identify areas for improvement and make data-driven decisions that enhance effectiveness.

Building Resilience

1. **Investing in Staff Development**: Offering professional development opportunities helps staff adapt to changing conditions while enhancing their skills.

2. **Creating a Supportive Environment**: Fostering a culture of psychological safety encourages staff to share concerns and innovate without fear of failure.

3. **Networking**: Non-profit leaders can benefit from establishing networks with peers and industry experts to exchange knowledge and resources, especially during uncertain times.

Ethical Leadership in Non-Profit Organizations

Upholding Ethical Standards

Ethical leadership is vital for maintaining the trust of stakeholders in non-profit organizations. Leaders must prioritize integrity, accountability, and transparency in all aspects of their work.

Strategies for Ethical Leadership

1. **Developing a Code of Ethics**: Establishing a formal code of ethics provides a framework for decision-making and organizational behavior, guiding staff in ethical dilemmas.

2. **Creating Accountability Structures**: Regular audits, performance evaluations, and transparency in decision-making processes reinforce ethical accountability within the organization.

3. **Promoting Whistleblower Policies**: Encouraging staff to report unethical behavior without fear of retaliation fosters a culture of integrity.

4. **Training on Ethical Issues**: Providing training and resources on ethical dilemmas equips staff with the knowledge needed to navigate complex situations.

Conclusion

Leadership in non-profit organizations requires a unique set of skills and qualities that reflect the missions and values of these entities. Purpose-driven leaders who articulate and communicate their organizations' missions effectively can inspire diverse stakeholders and drive engagement. Collaboration, relationship-building, and community involvement are foundational to creating a culture of support, while financial acumen and adaptability enable organizations to navigate challenges and ensure sustainability.

As the non-profit landscape continues to evolve, ethical leadership remains paramount, guiding organizations toward responsible practices that uphold stakeholder trust. By embodying these principles, leaders can cultivate impactful non-profits that contribute to positive change within their communities.

In the following chapters, we will explore leadership in other sectors, examining how the principles discussed here can be adapted and applied across diverse organizational contexts. The lessons learned in non-profit leadership can illuminate best practices for aspiring leaders in business and government, ultimately equipping them to drive meaningful change in their respective fields.

Chapter 4: Leadership in Sports

Introduction

Leadership in sports transcends the boundaries of games and competitions; it is about building teams, fostering resilience, and inspiring individuals to perform at their best, both on and off the field. Successful sports leaders are not only strategic thinkers and decision-makers but also effective communicators, motivators, and mentors. This chapter delves into the multifaceted nature of leadership in sports, examining the qualities that define effective sports leaders, the dynamics of team culture, the challenges faced in this arena, and the lessons that can be learned from both successful and unsuccessful leadership examples.

The Essence of Leadership in Sports

Defining Leadership in Sports

At its core, leadership in sports involves influencing and guiding athletes and teams toward achieving collective goals. Sports leaders—coaches, captains, and organizational executives—play a pivotal role in shaping the identity and ethos of a team. They harness the unique strengths, capabilities, and aspirations of their athletes to create a unified force that can overcome challenges and achieve success.

Key Qualities of Effective Sports Leaders

1. **Vision**: Effective leaders articulate a clear vision that inspires and motivates athletes. This vision outlines team goals and sets high but achievable standards for performance.

2. **Communication**: Sports leaders must communicate effectively, delivering instructions clearly and constructively. They should also actively listen to feedback from athletes to foster an environment of open dialogue.

3. **Empathy**: Understanding the emotional and psychological needs of athletes is vital. Leaders who foster a supportive atmosphere enhance team cohesion and individual well-being.

4. **Resilience**: Sports leaders must model resilience, demonstrating the ability to persevere through challenges, setbacks, and failures. Their approach to adversity can set the tone for the entire team.

5. **Integrity**: Ethical leadership is paramount in sports. Leaders should exemplify honesty and fairness, earning the respect and trust of their athletes through their actions.

The Leader-Athlete Dynamic

The effectiveness of a sports leader often hinges on their relationship with athletes. Leaders must foster trust and respect while maintaining authority in their role. This balance can be achieved through:

- **Empowerment**: Allowing athletes to take ownership of their performance fosters autonomy and accountability. Empowering athletes to contribute to decision-making processes enhances their investment in team goals.

- **Feedback and Recognition**: Providing timely, specific feedback helps athletes improve their skills. Celebrating both individual and team achievements reinforces a positive culture.

- **Building Rapport**: Invest time in understanding the personalities and backgrounds of athletes, developing strong relationships that extend beyond practices or games.

Cultivating Team Culture

The Importance of Team Culture

Team culture encompasses the shared values, beliefs, and practices that define a sports team. A strong positive culture is crucial for maximizing performance, enhancing motivation, and ensuring collective commitment to the team's goals.

Elements of a Positive Team Culture

1. **Shared Values**: Define and promote core values that every member of the team, from players to support staff, adheres to, fostering a sense of unity.

2. **Inclusivity**: Foster a culture that celebrates diversity, ensuring that all voices are valued and respected. Inclusivity drives collaboration and strengthens team bonds.

3. **Accountability**: Establish clear expectations for performance and behavior. A culture of accountability empowers athletes to take responsibility for their actions.

4. **Support and Camaraderie**: Encourage an environment where teammates support one another, both in practice and during challenging moments in competition.

5. **Continuous Learning**: Instill a growth mindset, promoting a culture of learning from mistakes and celebrating progress. Emphasizing improvement over perfection helps build resilience.

Engaging with Stakeholders

In addition to athletes, sports leaders interact with a range of stakeholders, including coaches, sponsors, fans, and media. Building strong relationships with these groups is critical to nurturing a positive team culture.

1. **Coaches**: Collaborative relationships with assistant coaches enable a cohesive approach to training and development.

2. **Fans**: Engaging with fans and fostering a sense of community can create a supportive atmosphere that bolsters team morale.

3. **Media**: Maintaining positive relationships with journalists can enhance the team's public image and manage narratives surrounding performance.

Challenges in Sports Leadership

Managing Performance Pressure

Sports leaders face immense pressure to perform, especially in professional and elite contexts. This pressure can stem from expectations of stakeholders, media scrutiny, and internal ambitions. Effective leaders must develop coping strategies to manage this stress constructively.

Strategy for Handling Performance Pressure

1. **Setting Realistic Goals**: While ambitions are important, leaders should set achievable short-term goals that contribute to larger objectives. This helps mitigate anxiety and enables athletes to focus on incremental progress.

2. **Encouraging Mental Resilience**: Training the mental toughness of athletes prepares them to handle performance pressures effectively. Emphasizing relaxation techniques, visualization, and mindfulness can enhance mental preparedness.

3. **Creating a Safe Space**: Foster an environment where athletes feel comfortable discussing stressors and fears without fear of judgment. Open dialogues around mental health are vital.

Navigating Conflicts

Conflict is an inevitable aspect of team dynamics, arising from differing personalities, competitive tensions, or management disagreements. Sports leaders must be adept at conflict resolution, ensuring that disputes are addressed constructively.

1. **Active Listening**: Facilitating conversations that allow each party to express their views fosters understanding and lays the groundwork for resolution.

2. **Mediation**: Neutral mediation between conflicting parties can help clarify issues and encourage collaborative problem-solving.

3. **Establishing Ground Rules**: Creating explicit behavioral expectations can mitigate conflict and set parameters for acceptable conduct within the team.

Learning from Leadership Examples

Successful Leadership Case Study: Phil Jackson

Phil Jackson, the legendary coach of the Chicago Bulls and Los Angeles Lakers, is often hailed as one of the greatest leaders in sports history. His successful leadership strategies included:

1. **Philosophy of Teamwork**: Jackson emphasized collective success over individual

accolades, promoting a culture of unselfish play and mutual support.

2. **Mindfulness and Psychological Techniques**: He integrated mindfulness practices into training, helping athletes develop mental resilience.

3. **Empowerment**: Jackson encouraged players to take ownership of their roles on the court, fostering a sense of autonomy in decision-making.

The combination of Jackson's leadership strategies cultivated championship-winning teams, illustrating the power of effective leadership in sports.

Lessons from Unsuccessful Leadership: Bobby Knight

Contrastingly, Bobby Knight's leadership style—marked by intense discipline and often aggressive tactics—has been both lauded for its results and criticized for its impact on team culture and player relationships.

1. **Intimidation Strategies**: Knight's use of humiliation led to toxic team dynamics that impacted athlete well-being and morale.

2. **Limited Communication**: His one-way communication approach stifled feedback from players, undermining trust.

3. **Failure to Adapt**: Knight's rigidity in tactics overlooked the individual personalities and needs of athletes, causing friction and disengagement.

These contrasting examples underscore the importance of adaptability, empathetic communication, and fostering strong relationships within a sports team.

Conclusion

Leadership in sports is a complex and dynamic endeavor that requires unique skills, qualities, and approaches. Effective leaders are visionaries who inspire athletes and cultivate a positive team culture centered on collaboration, accountability, and inclusion. They navigate the challenges of performance pressure, conflict, and stakeholder engagement, all while upholding ethical standards.

As we draw from both the successes and failures of notable figures in sports leadership, it becomes evident that successful leadership transcends winning games; it is about shaping resilient individuals and cohesive teams. The principles explored in this chapter not only apply to sports but can also inform leadership practices across various sectors. In the next chapter, we will continue our exploration of leadership in different contexts, uncovering further insights and lessons applicable to aspiring leaders in any field.

Chapter 5: Leadership in Healthcare

Introduction

Leadership in healthcare is critical to the delivery of high-quality care, the management of complex organizations, and the development of innovative solutions to pressing health challenges. As healthcare systems face unique pressures, ranging from regulatory changes and technological advancements to evolving patient expectations and public health crises, effective leadership has become increasingly essential. This chapter explores the complexities of leadership in healthcare, examining the roles and responsibilities of healthcare leaders, the challenges they face, and effective strategies for navigating this dynamic landscape.

The Role of Healthcare Leaders

Defining Healthcare Leadership

Healthcare leadership encompasses a wide range of roles, from hospital administrators and policy makers to clinicians and department heads. Effective healthcare leaders must possess a deep understanding of both clinical and operational aspects while being able to influence and inspire their teams to achieve shared objectives.

Key Responsibilities of Healthcare Leaders

1. **Strategic Vision and Direction**: Leaders must articulate a clear vision for the organization that aligns with patient care objectives, community needs, and overall health policy frameworks. This vision guides priorities and strategic initiatives.

2. **Resource Management**: Leaders are responsible for managing financial, human, and technological resources effectively. This includes budgeting, staffing, and ensuring the efficient use of technology to improve patient outcomes.

3. **Quality Improvement and Safety**: A primary focus for healthcare leaders is ensuring patient safety and the continuous improvement of care quality. They promote best practices through training, monitoring, and adaptive change management.

4. **Collaboration and Partnership**: Healthcare leaders must work collaboratively with diverse stakeholders, including medical staff, government agencies, community

organizations, and patients. Building partnerships can enhance resource sharing and promote comprehensive health solutions.

5. **Advocacy and Policy Development**: Leaders must advocate for effective health policies and practices that promote equitable care and address broader health determinants in their communities.

Essential Qualities of Effective Healthcare Leaders

1. **Emotional Intelligence**: Healthcare leaders should possess high emotional intelligence, enabling them to empathize with staff and patients, foster collaboration, and navigate challenging interpersonal dynamics.

2. **Adaptability**: The healthcare landscape is continuously evolving; therefore, leaders must be adaptable and open to change in response to new technologies, regulations, and patient needs.

3. **Communication Skills**: Effective communication is crucial in healthcare. Leaders must convey information clearly, ensuring that all stakeholders understand their roles, responsibilities, and organizational goals.

4. **Decision-Making Skills**: Healthcare leaders often confront complex, high-stakes decisions. An ability to analyze data, consider ethical implications, and make informed choices is essential.

5. **Visionary Thinking**: Leaders should be forward-thinking, anticipating future challenges and opportunities in healthcare and developing strategies to address them proactively.

Challenges Facing Healthcare Leaders

Navigating a Complex Regulatory Environment

Healthcare leaders operate in a highly regulated environment, subject to laws and policies at the local, state, and federal levels. Keeping up with changes in regulations while maintaining compliance can be daunting.

1. **Staying Informed**: Leaders must stay up to date with shifting regulations and industry standards, employing legal and compliance experts as necessary.

2. **Implementing Changes**: When new regulations arise, leaders must implement necessary changes efficiently while minimizing disruptions to patient care.

Managing Financial Pressures

Many healthcare organizations grapple with financial constraints due to rising operational costs, fluctuating reimbursement rates, and demands for improved services.

1. **Cost Management**: Leaders must balance cost containment with the need to provide high-quality care, often employing innovative strategies such as telemedicine and preventive care to reduce expenses.

2. **Revenue Diversification**: Exploring diverse revenue streams—from grants and partnerships to chronic care management—can enhance financial stability.

Addressing Workforce Challenges

Recruiting, retaining, and developing skilled healthcare professionals is a significant challenge, especially amid workforce shortages and increasing burnout.

1. **Creating Positive Work Environments**: Leaders should prioritize staff well-being, implementing initiatives to address burnout and fostering a supportive culture.

2. **Investing in Continuous Education**: Supporting ongoing training and professional

development can enhance staff satisfaction and retention.

3. **Promoting Diversity and Inclusion**: Actively recruiting diverse talent and fostering an inclusive workplace can improve team dynamics and innovation.

Leading During Crises

Healthcare leaders must be adept at crisis management, especially during public health emergencies, such as the COVID-19 pandemic.

1. **Crisis Communication**: Leaders must communicate transparently and frequently with staff, patients, and the community, addressing concerns and sharing updates.

2. **Crisis Planning and Response**: Developing comprehensive crisis response plans is essential for ensuring preparedness and minimizing disruption during a crisis.

Strategies for Effective Healthcare Leadership

Fostering a Culture of Patient-Centered Care

1. **Engaging Patients in Decision-Making**: Involving patients in their care decisions enhances satisfaction and promotes adherence to treatment plans.

2. **Implementing Feedback Mechanisms**: Actively seeking and responding to patient feedback helps organizations identify areas for improvement and enhances the overall patient experience.

Driving Quality Improvement Initiatives

1. **Data-Driven Decision-Making**: Leaders should leverage data analytics to assess care quality, identify trends, and implement evidence-based improvements.

2. **Team Collaboration**: Creating multidisciplinary teams focused on quality improvement fosters diverse perspectives and enhances problem-solving.

3. **Continuous Training**: Providing ongoing education and training for staff cultivates a culture of excellence and ensures adherence to best practices.

Building Resilient Teams

1. **Empowering Staff**: Enabling team members to assume leadership roles in their areas of expertise encourages innovation and promotes a sense of ownership.

2. **Recognizing Contributions**: Celebrating staff achievements and recognizing individual

contributions motivates employees and strengthens team cohesion.

3. **Providing Support**: Implementing well-being programs, including mental health resources and stress management training, fosters resilience and promotes a positive work culture.

Navigating Change

1. **Leading by Example**: Leaders should model adaptability and openness to change, demonstrating willingness to pivot strategies and embrace new ideas.

2. **Communicating Vision**: Clearly communicating the rationale for changes ensures that staff understands the benefits and goals of new initiatives.

3. **Involving Stakeholders**: Engaging stakeholders in change processes fosters buy-in and collaboration, facilitating smoother transitions.

Learning from Healthcare Leadership Case Studies

Successful Leadership Case Study: Dr. Paul Farmer

Dr. Paul Farmer, co-founder of Partners In Health, exemplified transformative leadership in healthcare. His approach included:

1. **Commitment to Global Health Equity**: Farmer dedicated his life to addressing health disparities, particularly in impoverished communities. He advocated for the integration of social justice into healthcare.

2. **Innovative Models of Care**: Farmer promoted collaborative care models, emphasizing the importance of community health workers in reaching marginalized populations effectively.

3. **Partnership with Communities**: Fostering strong partnerships with local communities ensured that healthcare solutions were culturally relevant and community-driven.

Farmer's visionary approach not only improved health outcomes but also brought attention to systemic inequalities in global health.

Lessons from Unsuccessful Leadership: Case of UnitedHealthcare's Executive Missteps

In contrast, the case of mismanagement at UnitedHealthcare, particularly during instances of billing disputes and provider relations issues, illustrates the pitfalls of healthcare leadership.

1. **Lack of Transparency and Communication**: Failure to communicate openly with stakeholders led to dissatisfaction among providers and patients alike, eroding trust.

2. **Inflexibility in Policy Changes**: Resistance to adapting policies based on feedback from healthcare providers contributed to service disruptions, frustrating all parties involved.

3. **Ignoring Patient-Centric Approaches**: A focus on profitability over patient care diminished the quality of service and fostered negative perceptions among patients, ultimately impacting the organization's reputation.

These contrasting examples underscore the necessity of transparency, flexibility, and a patient-centered approach in effective healthcare leadership.

Conclusion

Healthcare leadership plays a vital role in shaping the future of health systems, ensuring the delivery of high-quality care, and promoting health equity. As healthcare leaders navigate challenges such as regulatory changes, financial pressures, workforce dynamics, and crisis management, the qualities of emotional intelligence, strong communication skills, and adaptability become paramount.

By fostering a culture of patient-centered care, driving quality initiatives, building resilient teams, and learning from past experiences, healthcare leaders can create environments that promote excellence, innovation, and compassion. As we turn to the next chapter, we will explore leadership in education, drawing connections between various sectors while uncovering new perspectives that can inform and enhance our understanding of effective leadership.

Chapter 6: Leadership in Technology

Introduction

The technology sector is one of the most dynamic and rapidly evolving fields in the modern world. In an environment characterized by constant change, innovation, and competition, effective leadership in technology is crucial to harnessing potential and driving organizational success. This chapter explores the distinct challenges and opportunities technology leaders face, the key qualities that define effective leadership in the tech sector, and strategies for fostering a thriving culture of innovation and collaboration.

The Role of Technology Leaders

Defining Leadership in Technology

Leadership in technology encompasses a range of positions, from Chief Technology Officers (CTOs) and product managers to team leads and project managers. These leaders are responsible for guiding their teams through complex technical challenges, aligning technological strategy with business objectives, and navigating a landscape marked by rapid technological advancements.

Key Responsibilities of Technology Leaders

1. **Strategic Vision**: Technology leaders must develop a clear vision that reflects the organization's goals and aligns technological advancements with business strategy. This vision guides product development, resource allocation, and long-term planning.

2. **Innovation Management**: In a sector defined by change, leaders must cultivate an innovation-friendly environment that encourages creativity, experimentation, and the agile application of new technologies.

3. **Team Development**: Hiring, mentoring, and developing talent is crucial for building high-performing teams. Technology leaders must recognize individual strengths and foster team cohesion.

4. **Stakeholder Engagement**: Leaders must effectively communicate and engage with a diverse range of stakeholders, including team members, executives, customers, and partners, ensuring that technology solutions meet broader business needs.

5. **Risk Management**: In an industry rife with uncertainties—from cybersecurity threats to evolving customer behaviors—technology leaders must assess, mitigate, and navigate risks associated with technological initiatives.

Essential Qualities of Effective Technology Leaders

1. **Visionary Thinking**: Effective tech leaders anticipate market trends and emerging technologies, positioning their organizations to capitalize on opportunities and mitigate threats.

2. **Technical Expertise**: A solid understanding of technology, programming languages, software development processes, and industry standards is essential for informed decision-making.

3. **Adaptability and Agility**: Given the fast-paced nature of the tech industry, leaders must demonstrate flexibility and agility, adapting to evolving demands and embracing change.

4. **Collaborative Mindset**: Technology leaders should foster collaboration within and between teams, promoting interdisciplinary partnerships that enhance problem-solving.

5. **Effective Communication**: Clear, concise communication is vital for ensuring that team members and stakeholders understand technological initiatives, organizational goals, and project progress.

Challenges Facing Technology Leaders

Keeping Pace with Rapid Change

The technology landscape evolves at a breathtaking pace, driven by advances in artificial intelligence, data analytics, cloud computing, and other disruptive technologies. Keeping up with these changes presents significant challenges.

1. **Continuous Learning**: Technology leaders must prioritize their ongoing education, engaging with industry conferences, professional organizations, and online resources to stay informed.

2. **Encouraging Lifelong Learning**: Leaders should cultivate a culture that values learning and development among team members, encouraging them to embrace new skills and technologies.

Managing Diverse Teams

Technology projects often require collaboration across diverse teams composed of individuals with varying expertise, backgrounds, and perspectives. Effectively managing these teams can be challenging.

1. **Fostering Inclusion**: Leaders must prioritize inclusivity, ensuring that all voices are heard, valued, and respected within the team.

2. **Balancing Autonomy and Oversight**: Striking the right balance between empowering team members to take ownership of their work and providing necessary oversight is critical for maintaining productivity and accountability.

Navigating Organizational Politics

Technology leaders may face challenges related to organizational politics, competing priorities, and misalignment with other departments, particularly in larger organizations.

1. **Building Alliances**: Developing strong relationships with key stakeholders, including executives and leaders from other departments, can facilitate collaboration and align strategic objectives.

2. **Enhancing Visibility**: Technology leaders should advocate for the technical team's contributions and accomplishments, ensuring

that their impact is recognized throughout the organization.

Ensuring Cybersecurity

As reliance on technology increases, so too does the risk of cyber threats. Technology leaders must prioritize cybersecurity, safeguarding both organizational data and customer trust.

1. **Developing Robust Security Protocols**: Leaders should invest in comprehensive cybersecurity measures, including regular security audits, employee training, and response plans for potential breaches.

2. **Staying Informed on Threats**: Keeping abreast of emerging cybersecurity threats and industry best practices is essential for mitigating risk.

Strategies for Effective Technology Leadership

Fostering a Culture of Innovation

1. **Encouraging Creativity**: Leaders can create a safe environment for experimentation, where team members feel comfortable proposing novel ideas and solutions.

2. **Empowering Teams**: Autonomy inspires innovation. Leaders should empower their

teams by giving them ownership of projects and encouraging them to pursue creative solutions.

3. **Establishing Innovation Processes**: Leaders should implement structured processes for researching, evaluating, and integrating innovative ideas into the business model.

Embracing Agile Methodologies

1. **Implementing Agile Frameworks**: Adopting Agile methodologies, such as Scrum or Kanban, fosters flexibility, adaptability, and quick responses to changing requirements.

2. **Continuous Feedback Loops**: Leaders should facilitate regular feedback sessions to gather insights from team members and stakeholders, ensuring continuous improvement.

Prioritizing Team Development

1. **Investing in Professional Development**: Providing opportunities for skills development, training, and certifications encourages continuous growth and enhances team capabilities.

2. **Mentorship Programs**: Encouraging mentorship within the organization strengthens relationships, promotes knowledge sharing, and helps develop future technology leaders.

Enhancing Communication and Collaboration

1. **Utilizing Collaboration Tools**: Investing in tools that facilitate communication and collaboration enhances productivity and streamlines workflows among remote or cross-functional teams.

2. **Regular Check-Ins**: Establishing a rhythm of regular team meetings and one-on-one check-ins encourages open communication and allows leaders to address challenges proactively.

Building Resilience and Adaptability

1. **Scenario Planning**: Leaders should anticipate various potential scenarios, preparing their teams to pivot quickly when needed.

2. **Promoting a Growth Mindset**: Encouraging a growth mindset among team members fosters resilience in the face of setbacks and challenges.

Learning from Technology Leadership Case Studies

Successful Leadership Case Study: Satya Nadella at Microsoft

Satya Nadella's leadership at Microsoft serves as a prime example of transformative leadership in the technology sector. His approach embodies several critical strategies:

1. **Cultural Shift**: Nadella prioritized a cultural transformation at Microsoft, shifting from a "know-it-all" to a "learn-it-all" mindset, promoting collaboration, learning, and experimentation.

2. **Focus on Cloud Computing**: Under his leadership, Microsoft embraced cloud technologies, pivoting the company's strategy toward cloud-based solutions, which has significantly enhanced its market position.

3. **Empowerment and Inclusion**: Nadella emphasized diversity and inclusion, fostering a workforce that reflects a wide range of perspectives and backgrounds, which has been critical to driving innovation.

Nadella's vision and commitment to a growth-oriented culture have not only revitalized Microsoft but have also established it as a leader in emerging technology.

Lessons from Unsuccessful Leadership: Yahoo's Leadership Changes

In contrast, the frequent leadership changes at Yahoo during the 2010s illustrate the pitfalls of instability and lack of clear direction. Some of the contributing factors to Yahoo's decline included:

1. **Frequent Executive Turnover**: Rapid changes in leadership inhibited the establishment of a coherent strategy, resulting in confusion among employees and stakeholders.

2. **Failure to Adapt**: Yahoo struggled to pivot in response to changing industry trends, particularly in the face of competition from Google and Facebook, leading to lost market opportunities.

3. **Misalignment in Goals**: Inconsistent priorities and lack of a unified vision undermined the organization's ability to innovate and compete effectively in the tech landscape.

These contrasting examples highlight the importance of consistent leadership, a clear strategic vision, and a commitment to fostering innovation in technology organizations.

Conclusion

Leadership in technology is a multifaceted and dynamic role that demands a unique skill set and a forward-thinking mindset. Technology leaders must navigate challenges related to rapid change, team dynamics, organizational politics, and cybersecurity while inspiring their teams to innovate and excel. By fostering cultures of innovation, embracing flexible methodologies, prioritizing team development, enhancing communication, and building resilience, leaders can establish thriving technological environments that drive success.

As we transition to the next chapter, we will explore leadership in the nonprofit sector, uncovering insights and strategies that can inform and enhance leadership practices across diverse contexts, while also learning how the principles discussed can be applied to make meaningful impacts in society.

Chapter 7: Leadership in Government

Introduction

Leadership in government is a complex and vital component of modern society. As the stewards of public resources and the architects of policies that affect the lives of millions, government leaders face unique challenges and responsibilities. This chapter delves into the roles and qualities essential for effective leadership within government entities, examines the multifaceted challenges leaders encounter, and provides strategies to foster impactful governance in a changing world.

The Role of Government Leaders

Defining Leadership in Government

Government leadership encompasses various roles, from elected officials and government executives to civil servants and community leaders. These individuals are responsible for making critical decisions that shape public policy, uphold democratic values, and promote community welfare.

Key Responsibilities of Government Leaders

1. **Policy Development**: Government leaders are tasked with creating policies that address societal challenges, facilitate economic growth, and ensure public safety. They must engage with constituents and stakeholders to understand the needs of the community.

2. **Resource Allocation**: Leaders must manage public funds efficiently, ensuring that resources are allocated in a manner that maximizes impact while adhering to principles of transparency and accountability.

3. **Crisis Management**: Leaders must navigate crises, such as natural disasters, public health emergencies, or economic downturns, demonstrating decisive and effective leadership under pressure.

4. **Public Engagement**: Effective leaders promote engagement with citizens, fostering trust and ensuring that public voices are heard in the decision-making process.

5. **Advocacy for Social Justice**: Government leaders have a responsibility to advocate for policies that promote equality, address

systemic injustices, and support marginalized communities.

Essential Qualities of Effective Government Leaders

1. **Integrity**: Trustworthiness and adherence to ethical standards are foundational for government leaders, as they must maintain public trust to effectively govern.

2. **Visionary Thinking**: Leaders should possess a clear vision that aligns with the needs and aspirations of the community, guiding policy decisions and strategic initiatives.

3. **Emotional Intelligence**: The ability to understand and manage emotions, both their own and those of others, is critical for navigating complex interpersonal relationships and fostering collaboration.

4. **Political Acumen**: Navigating the political landscape requires an understanding of power dynamics, coalition building, and negotiation skills to achieve policy objectives effectively.

5. **Resilience**: Government leaders must be resilient, capable of adapting to challenges and setbacks while remaining committed to their vision and mission.

Challenges Facing Government Leaders

Navigating Bureaucracy

Government operations are often characterized by complex bureaucracies that can hinder responsiveness and innovation. Leaders must find ways to navigate these hurdles effectively.

1. **Streamlining Processes**: Leaders should advocate for process improvements and simplify workflows to enhance efficiency while maintaining accountability and oversight.

2. **Fostering a Culture of Innovation**: Encouraging creativity and flexibility within government organizations can help overcome bureaucratic inertia and improve service delivery.

Engaging with Diverse Stakeholders

Government leaders must interact with a variety of stakeholders, including citizens, advocacy groups, businesses, and other government entities. Balancing these diverse interests can be challenging.

1. **Building Relationships**: Establishing strong relationships with stakeholders and actively seeking input fosters collaboration, enhances trust, and leads to better-informed policy decisions.

2. **Conflict Resolution**: Leaders must hone their conflict resolution skills, navigating disagreements and finding common ground among diverse interests to facilitate progress.

Ensuring Accountability and Transparency

In an era characterized by heightened scrutiny and demand for accountability, government leaders must ensure transparency in their actions and decisions.

1. **Implementing Transparency Measures**: Leaders should establish and promote transparent processes that allow for public oversight and scrutiny of government actions.

2. **Encouraging Citizen Participation**: Actively seeking citizen input into policy development processes fosters a sense of ownership among constituents and enhances accountability.

Adapting to Technological Change

As technology continues to reshape governance, leaders must adapt to new digital tools while addressing concerns related to data privacy and cybersecurity.

1. **Investing in Technology**: Leaders should prioritize investment in technology that improves service delivery and enhances

citizen engagement, ensuring that public services are accessible and efficient.

2. **Cybersecurity Awareness**: Understanding and addressing cybersecurity risks is critical for government leaders to protect sensitive information and maintain public trust.

Strategies for Effective Government Leadership

Cultivating a Collaborative Culture

1. **Encouraging Cross-Department Collaboration**: Promoting collaboration among different departments and levels of government can lead to more holistic and effective policy solutions.

2. **Empowering Employees**: Encouraging civil servants to take initiative and contribute ideas fosters a sense of ownership and enhances employee engagement.

Prioritizing Communication

1. **Transparent Communication Channels**: Establishing clear, accessible communication channels between government leaders and the public enhances transparency and trust.

2. **Utilizing Technology**: Leveraging social media and other digital tools can help government leaders reach broader audiences, disseminate information, and engage with citizens effectively.

Fostering Inclusivity

1. **Promoting Diversity in Leadership**: Ensuring diverse representation within leadership roles enhances perspectives and improves policy outcomes.

2. **Addressing Systemic Barriers**: Actively working to eliminate barriers to participation and advocating for marginalized communities builds a more just and equitable society.

Emphasizing Continuous Learning

1. **Investing in Training and Development**: Government leaders should prioritize professional development opportunities for themselves and their teams to promote effective leadership and enhanced skills.

2. **Learning from Experience**: Reflecting on past successes and failures provides valuable insights that can improve future decision-making and governance practices.

Learning from Government Leadership Case Studies

Successful Leadership Case Study: Jacinda Ardern, Prime Minister of New Zealand

Jacinda Ardern's leadership exemplifies effective governance characterized by empathy, decisiveness, and inclusivity:

1. **Crisis Management**: Ardern's response to the Christchurch mosque shootings demonstrated strong leadership through compassion and decisive action, as she quickly implemented gun control measures and emphasized unity and tolerance.

2. **Public Engagement**: Ardern consistently engaged with citizens through transparent communication, particularly during the COVID-19 pandemic, fostering trust and promoting adherence to public health measures.

3. **Focus on Well-being**: Her government has prioritized a well-being approach to policy-making, advocating for holistic measures that go beyond traditional economic indicators.

Ardern's empathetic and proactive leadership has garnered international recognition and demonstrates the power of compassionate governance.

Lessons from Unsuccessful Leadership: The Flint Water Crisis

The Flint water crisis serves as a cautionary tale regarding government leadership and accountability:

1. **Failure to Respond to Public Concerns**: Government officials' failure to heed warnings from citizens about water quality led to a public health disaster. This illustrates the importance of active listening and engagement with the community.

2. **Lack of Transparency**: The withholding of information about the water crisis from the public undermined trust and accountability, exacerbating the situation and leading to significant health consequences.

3. **Systemic Inequalities**: The crisis highlighted systemic issues of race and socio-economic inequality, demonstrating the importance of addressing social justice concerns in governance.

The Flint water crisis underscores the critical importance of accountability, transparency, and community engagement in effective government leadership.

Conclusion

Leadership in government is a multifaceted and essential role that demands a unique blend of skills, integrity, and a commitment to public service. As government leaders navigate challenges such as bureaucracy, stakeholder engagement, accountability, and technological change, they must foster collaborative cultures, prioritize effective communication, promote inclusivity, and embrace continuous learning.

Drawing lessons from both successful and unsuccessful leadership examples enhances our understanding of effective governance. As we move to the next chapter, we will explore leadership in the field of education, uncovering how leadership principles can be applied to foster impactful learning environments and empower future generations.

Chapter 8: Leadership in the Arts

Introduction

Leadership in the arts is a unique and multifaceted endeavor that combines creativity, vision, and a deep understanding of cultural dynamics. Whether in the realms of music, theater, visual arts, or literature, artistic leaders play a crucial role in shaping creative expression, nurturing talent, and building community resilience. This chapter explores the distinct responsibilities and qualities of effective arts leaders, the challenges they face, and strategies for fostering innovation and collaboration within the artistic landscape.

The Role of Arts Leaders

Defining Leadership in the Arts

Arts leaders may take many forms, from artistic directors and curators to musicians, choreographers, and community organizers. Their roles often encompass not only guiding creative vision but also advocating for the arts, managing organizations, and engaging with diverse audiences.

Key Responsibilities of Arts Leaders

1. **Vision and Artistic Direction**: Arts leaders are responsible for developing and communicating a compelling artistic vision that guides an organization's work and resonates with its audience.

2. **Talent Development**: Nurturing artists, performers, and creative professionals is a critical aspect of leadership in the arts. This involves mentoring emerging talents, providing training opportunities, and fostering an environment conducive to creativity.

3. **Community Engagement**: Building relationships with the community and encouraging public participation in the arts are vital aspects of arts leadership. Engaging diverse audiences helps to enrich the cultural fabric of society.

4. **Resource Management**: Arts leaders must navigate the complexities of budgeting, fundraising, and resource allocation, ensuring the sustainability of their organizations while promoting creative endeavors.

5. **Advocacy and Cultural Policy**: Effective arts leaders advocate for the importance of the arts within society, influencing cultural policy, funding decisions, and public perception of the arts.

Essential Qualities of Effective Arts Leaders

1. **Creativity**: A strong creative vision is essential for arts leaders, who must not only inspire others but also innovate in the way that artistic work is produced and presented.

2. **Passion**: Genuine enthusiasm for the arts motivates leaders and their teams, helping to draw in audiences and sustain engagement over time.

3. **Collaboration**: The ability to bring together diverse voices and foster collaboration among artists, staff, and community members is crucial for successful artistic endeavors.

4. **Cultural Competence**: A deep understanding of cultural contexts and sensitivities allows arts leaders to engage authentically and respectfully with diverse communities.

5. **Resilience**: The ability to navigate challenges, overcome setbacks, and adapt to changing circumstances is essential for

sustaining artistic initiatives and organizations.

Challenges Facing Arts Leaders

Navigating Funding and Resource Limitations

The arts often face financial constraints, making fundraising and resource allocation a significant challenge for leaders.

1. **Dependence on External Funding**: Arts organizations typically rely on grants, sponsorships, and donations, necessitating effective fundraising strategies and relationship-building with potential funders.

2. **Economic Uncertainties**: Economic downturns can adversely impact arts funding, requiring leaders to think creatively about sustaining their organizations through tough times.

Fostering Inclusivity and Diversity

Inclusivity and diversity within the arts are essential for representative and authentic artistic expression but can pose challenges for leaders.

1. **Addressing Systemic Barriers**: Arts leaders must confront systemic inequalities

that affect access to opportunities for artists from marginalized communities.

2. **Building Diverse Audiences**: Engaging a wide range of audiences and participants ensures a richer cultural experience, but requires intentional strategies to reach diverse populations.

Balancing Artistic Vision with Practical Considerations

Arts leaders must often navigate the tension between artistic ambition and practical constraints.

1. **Compromise and Flexibility**: Leaders should be prepared to adapt their vision to meet logistical realities without compromising the core creative intent of projects.

2. **Integrating Feedback**: Actively seeking input from artists, audiences, and collaborators can aid leaders in refining their visions while accommodating practical considerations.

Establishing Long-term Sustainability

Long-term sustainability is a significant concern for arts organizations, particularly in a rapidly changing cultural landscape.

1. **Developing Strategic Plans**: Arts leaders should create and implement strategic plans that outline long-term goals, revenue models, and audience engagement strategies.

2. **Embracing Innovation**: Innovating in programming, outreach, and audience engagement can help organizations remain relevant and sustainable in an evolving environment.

Strategies for Effective Leadership in the Arts

Fostering a Collaborative Environment

1. **Encouraging Artistic Collaboration**: Facilitating collaboration among artists can lead to innovative projects and enriched creative experiences, promoting a sense of community within the arts.

2. **Building Interdisciplinary Partnerships**: Collaborating with organizations across disciplines, such as education, community services, and business, can extend the reach and impact of artistic initiatives.

Enhancing Community Engagement

1. **Creating Accessible Programs**: Developing programs that are accessible to diverse

audiences fosters participation and helps demystify the arts for the community.

2. **Leveraging Technology**: Utilizing digital tools and platforms can expand access to the arts, allowing broader engagement with a variety of audiences.

Prioritizing Diversity and Inclusion

1. **Implementing Inclusive Practices**: Arts leaders should actively work to ensure that their organizations reflect the diversity of the communities they serve in both programming and leadership roles.

2. **Investing in Community Dialogues**: Engaging in meaningful dialogues with community members helps to understand their needs and interests, informing more inclusive programming.

Emphasizing Professional Development

1. **Supporting Lifelong Learning**: Creating opportunities for continuous skill development for both artists and staff encourages ongoing growth and innovation within the organization.

2. **Establishing Mentorship Programs**: Pairing emerging artists with seasoned

professionals can foster knowledge sharing and build future leadership in the arts.

Advocating for Arts and Culture

1. **Building Alliances**: Creating partnerships with other arts organizations, community leaders, and advocacy groups amplifies the arts community's voice and influence.

2. **Engaging with Policymakers**: Advocating for favorable policies and funding for the arts requires building strong relationships with local, state, and national policymakers.

Learning from Leadership Case Studies in the Arts

Successful Leadership Case Study: Lin-Manuel Miranda

Lin-Manuel Miranda's contributions to theater and the arts illustrate the transformative power of leadership combined with creativity:

1. **Innovative Artistic Vision**: Miranda's groundbreaking musical *Hamilton* redefined the musical theater landscape by blending hip-hop, diverse casting, and historical narratives, captivating a wide audience.

2. **Community Engagement**: His commitment to community engagement is evident through initiatives like #EduHam, which offers educational performances of *Hamilton* for students, fostering interest in history and the arts.

3. **Advocacy for the Arts**: Miranda's advocacy extends beyond his work; he actively champions arts education and funding, emphasizing the importance of the arts for societal growth and individual empowerment.

Miranda's multifaceted leadership demonstrates how passion and creativity can foster impactful artistic expression and community connection.

Lessons from Unsuccessful Leadership: The Collapse of the American Conservatory Theater (ACT)

The challenges faced by the American Conservatory Theater (ACT) during financial turmoil highlight critical lessons in arts leadership:

1. **Failure to Adapt**: ACT struggled to adapt its programming and business model to changing audience preferences, leading to decreased ticket sales and financial instability.

2. **Lack of Community Engagement**: Insufficient outreach and engagement efforts

contributed to disconnection from its local community, diminishing support and relevance.

3. **Governance Issues**: Leadership turnover and internal discord hindered decision-making processes, leading to strategic misalignment and lack of coherent vision.

The ACT case underscores the importance of innovation, community engagement, and stable governance in sustaining arts organizations.

Conclusion

Leadership in the arts is an intricate interplay of creativity, collaboration, and community engagement. Effective arts leaders must navigate funding challenges, promote inclusivity, balance artistic vision with practical considerations, and ensure long-term sustainability. By fostering collaborative environments, prioritizing diversity, and engaging with communities, arts leaders can cultivate vibrant artistic ecosystems that enrich society.

As we transition to the next chapter, we will explore leadership in sports, examining how the principles discussed in the arts can inspire effective leadership in competitive and cooperative athletic environments, and uncovering the connections between creativity, resilience, and team dynamics.

Chapter 9: Leadership in Social Justice

Introduction

Leadership in social justice is about striving for equity, advocating for marginalized communities, and working toward systemic change. In a world marked by inequality and discrimination, social justice leaders play a transformative role in fostering a culture of inclusivity, empowerment, and accountability. This chapter delves into the essential responsibilities and attributes of effective social justice leaders, the challenges they encounter, and strategies for navigating the complexities of advocacy and activism in pursuit of a more equitable society.

The Role of Social Justice Leaders

Defining Leadership in Social Justice

Social justice leadership encompasses a diverse range of individuals, including activists, educators, community organizers, policymakers, and nonprofit executives. These leaders are united by a common goal: to dismantle systems of oppression and advocate for the rights and dignity of all individuals, particularly those marginalized by race, gender, sexuality, disability, and socio-economic status.

Key Responsibilities of Social Justice Leaders

1. **Advocacy and Activism**: Social justice leaders mobilize communities around issues of inequality and injustice, advocating for policy changes, raising awareness, and driving grassroots movements that call for action.

2. **Education and Awareness**: Leaders work to educate individuals and communities about social justice issues, facilitating difficult conversations and challenging prevailing narratives that perpetuate inequality.

3. **Building Coalitions**: Effective social justice leaders foster collaboration among diverse groups, recognizing that collective action amplifies impact and creates more comprehensive solutions to societal challenges.

4. **Empowerment and Capacity Building**: Leaders should empower marginalized communities by providing resources, training, and support that enable individuals to advocate for themselves and their rights.

5. **Accountability and Transparency**: Holding institutions, organizations, and leaders accountable for their actions and policies is essential in promoting ethical practices and nurturing a culture of justice.

Essential Qualities of Effective Social Justice Leaders

1. **Commitment to Equity**: A deep-seated commitment to fairness and justice is fundamental for social justice leaders, who must prioritize equity in their actions, decisions, and policies.

2. **Cultural Competence**: Understanding and respecting the diverse backgrounds and experiences of individuals is crucial for effective engagement and advocacy.

3. **Emotional Intelligence**: The ability to empathize with others, remain aware of one's emotions, and navigate complex social dynamics is vital for fostering trust and collaboration.

4. **Resilience and Persistence**: Social justice work is often met with resistance and setbacks. Resilience allows leaders to persevere in the face of challenges and maintain their commitment to change.

5. **Strategic Thinking**: Leaders must be capable of developing and implementing strategies that effectively address social issues, mobilize communities, and create meaningful change.

Challenges Facing Social Justice Leaders

Navigating Resistance and Pushback

Social justice leaders often face significant resistance from those invested in maintaining the status quo.

1. **Opposition from Institutions**: Established institutions may resist policy changes or reforms aimed at promoting social justice, necessitating strategic approaches to advocacy.

2. **Public Skepticism**: Leaders may encounter skepticism or indifference from the public regarding social justice issues, requiring skills in communication and persuasion to foster understanding and engagement.

Balancing Competing Interests

Social justice leaders must navigate competing interests within their movements and communities, which can create tension and conflict.

1. **Fostering Consensus**: Achieving a unified vision for action among diverse groups necessitates effective communication, negotiation skills, and an understanding of differing perspectives.

2. **Addressing Intersectionality**: Social justice issues are often interconnected; leaders must consider the complexities of intersectionality and ensure that the voices of the most marginalized are prioritized.

Resource Limitations

Many social justice initiatives depend on limited resources, which can constrain their ability to effect change.

1. **Funding Challenges**: Securing financial support for initiatives and organizations is often a continuous struggle, requiring innovative fundraising strategies and awareness campaigns.

2. **Capacity Building**: Leaders must focus on building the capacity of their organizations and communities, ensuring that they have the skills and resources necessary to pursue their objectives.

Maintaining Momentum and Engagement

Sustaining energy and engagement over the long term is critical for social justice efforts.

1. **Preventing Burnout**: The emotionally taxing nature of social justice work can lead to activist burnout. Leaders should prioritize self-care and wellness within their teams.

2. **Engaging New Voices**: Continuously attracting and mobilizing new supporters and activists is essential for maintaining momentum, particularly with changing societal trends and issues.

Strategies for Effective Leadership in Social Justice

Building Inclusive Communities

1. **Encouraging Diverse Participation**: Actively seeking to involve individuals from diverse backgrounds in social justice initiatives ensures a broader range of perspectives and experiences are considered.

2. **Creating Safe Spaces**: Leaders should foster inclusive environments where individuals feel safe sharing their stories and contributions.

Engaging in Advocacy and Policy Change

1. **Strategic Grassroots Campaigns**: Leaders can mobilize grassroots campaigns that focus on specific issues, building support and fostering community engagement through direct action.

2. **Lobbying and Policy Influence**: Engaging with policymakers and advocating for legislative change is essential for addressing systemic inequities.

Promoting Education and Awareness

1. **Facilitating Workshops and Trainings**: Providing educational opportunities for community members fosters awareness and equips individuals with the knowledge and skills needed for advocacy.

2. **Utilizing Digital Platforms**: Leveraging social media and other digital tools can raise awareness of social justice issues and connect individuals across geographical boundaries.

Nurturing Collaboration and Coalitions

1. **Building Bridges Among Organizations**: Collaborating with other social justice organizations enhances impact and fosters a spirit of solidarity.

2. **Creating Interdisciplinary Networks**: Engaging with leaders in other fields—such as education, healthcare, or environmental justice—can create holistic approaches to complex societal issues.

Embracing Cultural Competence and Sensitivity

1. **Incorporating Intersectionality**: Understanding how different forms of identity and oppression intersect allows leaders to develop solutions that address the unique challenges faced by marginalized communities.

2. **Engaging in Cultural Humility**: Leaders should approach their work with humility, recognizing that community members are experts in their own experiences and should be at the forefront of advocacy efforts.

Learning from Leadership Case Studies in Social Justice

Successful Leadership Case Study: Bryan Stevenson

Bryan Stevenson, a prominent lawyer and social justice advocate, exemplifies effective leadership in the fight for criminal justice reform:

1. **Vision and Advocacy**: Stevenson founded the Equal Justice Initiative (EJI), which provides legal representation to those who have been unfairly treated by the criminal justice system, focusing on marginalized populations.

2. **Storytelling as a Tool for Change**: Understanding the power of narrative, Stevenson shares compelling stories of those harmed by injustice, bringing attention to systemic failings and engaging audiences emotionally.

3. **Educational Outreach**: EJI has also prioritized education, creating a museum and memorial that raise awareness about the history of racial inequality and injustice in America, helping to inform public discourse.

Stevenson's multifaceted approach highlights the significance of advocacy, education, and storytelling in the pursuit of social justice.

Lessons from Unsuccessful Leadership: The Ferguson Protests

The protests that erupted in Ferguson, Missouri, following the police shooting of Michael Brown in 2014 reveal important lessons and challenges in social justice leadership:

1. **Fragmentation of Movements**: The widespread protests were marked by a lack of coordinated messaging or leadership, resulting in conflicting goals and strategies that diluted impact.

2. **Challenges of Sustained Engagement**: While initial outrage galvanized a movement, maintaining momentum over time proved difficult, highlighting the need for ongoing engagement and outreach efforts.

3. **Media Representation**: The portrayal of protesters in the media often focused on violence and unrest, overshadowing the underlying issues and narratives that fueled the protests.

These lessons underscore the necessity of clear messaging, sustained engagement, and strategic leadership within social movements.

Conclusion

Leadership in social justice is a vital and dynamic role that demands commitment, resilience, and collaboration. Social justice leaders advocate for equity, empower marginalized communities, and hold institutions accountable for their actions. By building inclusive communities, promoting education, engaging in advocacy, and nurturing collaboration, leaders can create pathways toward systemic change.

As we transition to the next chapter, we will explore leadership in environmental sustainability, uncovering how intersectionality and social justice principles impact efforts to protect our planet and ensure a just transition for all communities. The connections between social justice and environmental leadership shed light on the holistic nature of leadership and its potential to drive systemic change across multiple dimensions of society.

Chapter 10: Leadership in Environmentalism

Introduction

In an era marked by climate change, ecological degradation, and social inequities, leadership in environmentalism has never been more critical. Environmental leaders are tasked with navigating complex challenges that intersect with societal, economic, and political systems. This chapter explores the essential roles and responsibilities of leaders in the environmental movement, the challenges they face, and the strategies they employ to inspire change and foster sustainable practices for the planet and future generations.

The Role of Environmental Leaders

Defining Leadership in Environmentalism

Environmental leadership encompasses a wide variety of individuals and groups working to protect natural resources, promote sustainable practices, and advocate for policies that address environmental justice. These leaders can include scientists, activists, community organizers, policymakers, and business entrepreneurs committed to sustainable development.

Key Responsibilities of Environmental Leaders

1. **Advocacy for Policy Change**: Environmental leaders seek to influence public policy by advocating for legislation and regulations that protect ecosystems, reduce carbon emissions, and support sustainable practices.

2. **Education and Awareness**: Leaders play a crucial role in educating the public about environmental issues, fostering awareness of ecological challenges, and inspiring collective action.

3. **Sustainable Practices Promotion**: Encouraging businesses, communities, and individuals to adopt sustainable practices, from waste reduction to renewable energy use, is central to environmental leadership.

4. **Restoration and Conservation**: Leaders often oversee projects that restore damaged ecosystems, protect endangered species, and promote biodiversity to ensure the health of the planet.

5. **Building Resilient Communities**: Environmental leaders work to empower communities to adapt to climate change, focusing on resilience strategies that mitigate environmental impacts and enhance social equity.

Essential Qualities of Effective Environmental Leaders

1. **Visionary Thinking**: Effective environmental leaders possess a long-term vision for sustainability, balancing immediate needs with the protection of future resources and ecological health.

2. **Passion and Commitment**: A genuine passion for the environment and a commitment to promoting ecological sustainability drive leaders to take action and motivate others.

3. **Interdisciplinary Knowledge**: An understanding of various fields—science, economics, sociology, and policy—enables leaders to develop holistic approaches to environmental challenges.

4. **Collaboration and Inclusiveness**: Fostering partnerships and engaging multiple stakeholders, including marginalized

communities, is vital in creating inclusive and effective environmental strategies.

5. **Adaptability and Resilience**: The dynamic nature of environmental issues requires leaders to be adaptable and resilient, willing to pivot strategies in response to new information or changing circumstances.

Challenges Facing Environmental Leaders

Climate Change and Ecological Threats

Environmental leaders face the immense challenge of combating climate change and its far-reaching effects, which include extreme weather events, sea-level rise, and biodiversity loss.

1. **Data and Communication Gaps**: Misinformation and lack of public understanding about climate science can hinder efforts to mobilize communities and build political will.

2. **Systemic Barriers**: Existing political, social, and economic systems often prioritize short-term gains over long-term sustainability, making it difficult for leaders to enact necessary changes.

Resource Limitations

The availability of funding and resources is a significant challenge for many environmental initiatives.

1. **Competition for Grants**: Nonprofits and grassroots organizations often face fierce competition for limited funding, making it challenging to sustain long-term projects.

2. **Infrastructure Limitations**: In many communities, inadequate infrastructure for recycling, waste management, and renewable energy can impede sustainable practices.

Engaging Communities and Stakeholders

Fostering community engagement and collaboration among diverse stakeholders is crucial yet challenging.

1. **Overcoming Political Polarization**: Environmental issues are often politicized, requiring leaders to navigate differing viewpoints and foster dialogue among conflicting groups.

2. **Cultural Sensitivity**: Leaders must be sensitive to diverse cultural perspectives and values regarding environmental stewardship to create inclusive programs and initiatives.

Maintaining Public Momentum

Sustaining public interest and engagement in environmental causes can be difficult, particularly amidst competing priorities.

1. **Preventing Activist Burnout**: The emotional toll of addressing climate change can lead to burnout among environmental activists, necessitating strategies to promote wellness and resilience.

2. **Long-term Engagement Strategies**: Keeping individuals involved in environmental causes over the long haul requires innovative approaches to advocacy and community-building.

Strategies for Effective Leadership in Environmentalism

Building Strong Coalitions

1. **Partnership Development**: Building coalitions with nonprofits, government agencies, businesses, and local communities can amplify impact and share resources effectively.

2. **Inclusive Engagement**: Creating space for diverse voices ensures that solutions reflect the needs and priorities of various

communities, fostering a sense of ownership in environmental initiatives.

Advocating for Sustainable Policy

1. **Lobbying for Change**: Environmental leaders can engage in lobbying efforts, working with legislators to push for robust environmental policies at local, national, and international levels.

2. **Public Mobilization**: Organizing campaigns and movements that elevate public consciousness and encourage civic engagement is essential for driving policy change.

Promoting Education and Awareness

1. **Community Workshops and Events**: Organizing educational events and workshops can engage communities in learning and discussion around environmental issues and solutions.

2. **Utilizing Digital Tools**: Leveraging social media platforms and online campaigns can broaden outreach efforts and connect individuals who are passionate about environmental justice.

Implementing Sustainable Practices

1. **Showcase Local Solutions**: Highlighting successful local sustainability initiatives can inspire others and provide practical models that can be replicated.

2. **Corporate Partnerships**: Engaging businesses to adopt sustainable practices through corporate social responsibility initiatives can drive meaningful change in consumption patterns and resource management.

Fostering Resilience and Adaptability

1. **Community Resilience Plans**: Leaders should help communities develop plans that address climate vulnerability, ensuring that responses are context-specific and culturally appropriate.

2. **Research and Development**: Encouraging innovation in sustainable technology and practices can drive forward-thinking solutions that address emerging environmental challenges.

Learning from Leadership Case Studies in Environmentalism

Successful Leadership Case Study: Jane Goodall

Jane Goodall, renowned for her groundbreaking work with chimpanzees, exemplifies transformative leadership in environmentalism:

1. **Research and Conservation**: Goodall's extensive research on chimps in Tanzania led to a greater understanding of animal behavior and conservation needs, illustrating the critical nexus of science and advocacy.

2. **Community Engagement**: Through her organization, the Jane Goodall Institute, she has integrated community development, conservation, and education, focusing on grassroots efforts that support both people and wildlife.

3. **Global Advocacy**: Goodall's global outreach efforts emphasize the importance of youth involvement in conservation, mobilizing new generations to take action for environmental sustainability.

Goodall's multifaceted approach showcases the powerful intersection of research, advocacy, and community-building in environmental leadership.

Lessons from Unsuccessful Leadership: The Cape Town Water Crisis

The Cape Town water crisis in South Africa highlights the complexities of environmental leadership and crisis management:

1. **Inadequate Preparedness**: Failure to adequately prepare for water scarcity due to climate change, mismanagement, and population growth led to severe shortages.

2. **Communication Breakdown**: A lack of clear communication regarding water-saving measures and crisis management eroded public trust and resulted in confusion among residents.

3. **Equity Issues**: The crisis disproportionately affected marginalized communities, emphasizing the need for inclusive strategies that address equity and access to resources.

The lessons from this crisis illustrate the importance of proactive planning, effective communication, and prioritizing equity in environmental leadership.

Conclusion

Leadership in environmentalism is an essential component of creating a sustainable future for our planet. Environmental leaders advocate for policy change, educate communities, promote sustainable practices, and build coalitions to address ecological challenges. By employing strategies that emphasize inclusivity, resilience, and innovation, environmental leaders can mobilize individuals and communities to pursue systemic changes that benefit both people and the planet.

As we transition to the concluding chapter, we will explore the interconnectedness of various leadership arenas—examining how insights from the arts, social justice, and environmentalism can inform and inspire holistic leadership practices across diverse fields. This exploration will highlight the potential for interdisciplinary collaboration in solving the pressing issues of our time, reinforcing the importance of visionary leadership in fostering a healthier, more equitable, and sustainable world.

Chapter 11: Leadership in Family Dynamics

Introduction

Family dynamics play a crucial role in shaping individual identities, beliefs, and behaviors. As the primary social unit, families not only provide emotional support but also serve as the first environment where leadership principles are learned and practiced. Leadership within families involves guiding, supporting, and nurturing each member while managing relationships effectively. This chapter explores the essential qualities and strategies of leadership in family dynamics, the challenges families face, and the developmental and relational opportunities that arise from effective family leadership.

The Role of Family Leaders

Defining Leadership in Family Dynamics

Leadership in a family context refers to the ability to guide, influence, and support family members in a way that promotes healthy relationships, individual growth, and collective well-being. Family leaders can be parents, guardians, or even children who take on leadership roles within their households; these leaders foster an environment of love, respect, and mutual support.

Key Responsibilities of Family Leaders

1. **Instilling Values and Beliefs**: Family leaders are responsible for promoting core values, instilling beliefs, and modeling desired behaviors that shape the family culture.

2. **Effective Communication**: Open and honest communication is vital for fostering understanding and connection among family members. Leaders must create an environment where everyone feels safe to express their thoughts and feelings.

3. **Conflict Resolution**: Family leaders must navigate conflicts and disagreements constructively, facilitating discussions that lead to resolution and deeper understanding.

4. **Providing Support and Guidance**: Offering emotional support and guidance during challenging times is essential in helping family members develop resilience and nurture their personal growth.

5. **Cultivating Teamwork**: Family leaders encourage collaboration and teamwork, ensuring that all family members work together towards common goals and shared responsibilities.

Essential Qualities of Effective Family Leaders

1. **Empathy and Sensitivity**: Understanding and relating to the emotions and needs of family members fosters a sense of belonging and support.

2. **Flexibility and Adaptability**: Family dynamics can shift due to life changes, growth phases, or external factors. Effective leaders adapt to these changes while maintaining stability.

3. **Consistency and Reliability**: Providing a steady, reliable presence helps family members feel secure and supported.

4. **Visionary Thinking**: Effective family leaders have a vision for their family, prioritizing long-term goals and aspirations

while balancing immediate needs and challenges.

5. **Encouragement and Celebration**: Leaders recognize and celebrate family members' accomplishments, fostering a culture of encouragement and motivation.

Challenges Facing Family Leaders

Navigating Change and Transitions

Families go through numerous transitions, such as the arrival of new children, aging, divorce, or loss. These changes can significantly impact family dynamics.

1. **Adaptation to Change**: Family leaders must help navigate the emotional upheaval that accompanies major life transitions, supporting family members as they adjust.

2. **Reassessing Roles and Responsibilities**: Changes in family structure or dynamics require leaders to reassess individual roles, ensuring that all members feel valued and included.

Managing Conflicts and Disagreements

Conflict is a natural aspect of family life, but it can lead to tension and dysfunction if not managed effectively.

1. **Emotional Intensity**: Family disagreements can evoke strong emotions, complicating the resolution process. Leaders must remain calm and constructive in their approach.

2. **Diverse Perspectives**: Each family member may have a unique perspective on conflicts, necessitating sensitive negotiation and compromise.

Balancing Multiple Roles

Family leaders often juggle various responsibilities outside the family unit—such as work, community involvement, and personal health—which can lead to stress and fragmentation.

1. **Time Management**: Balancing professional commitments with family needs requires effective time management and prioritization.

2. **Self-Care**: Leaders must remember to prioritize their well-being to maintain their ability to support their families effectively.

Addressing External Pressures

Families often encounter external pressures from societal expectations, economic factors, and cultural norms.

1. **Social Expectations**: Family leaders may feel pressured to conform to societal norms regarding parenting or marriage, which can create tension and lead to feelings of inadequacy.

2. **Economic Stressors**: Financial challenges can exacerbate family stress, affecting relationships and overall well-being.

Strategies for Effective Leadership in Family Dynamics

Promoting Open Communication

1. **Regular Family Meetings**: Holding regular meetings encourages open dialogue, allowing family members to voice concerns, share achievements, and discuss collective goals.

2. **Active Listening**: Cultivating active listening skills ensures that each family member feels heard and valued, fostering mutual respect.

Cultivating Relationships and Bonds

1. **Quality Time**: Prioritizing family time through activities, traditions, or shared meals strengthens connections and builds positive memories.

2. **Supportive Environment**: Creating an atmosphere of trust and encouragement allows family members to express themselves freely and seek help without fear of judgment.

Implementing Conflict Resolution Techniques

1. **Establishing Ground Rules**: Setting guidelines for discussions can help maintain respect and civility during conflicts, encouraging a collaborative approach to resolution.

2. **Use of "I" Statements**: Encouraging family members to express their feelings proactively helps de-escalate tensions and prevents blame-casting.

Delegating Responsibilities

1. **Division of Labor**: Assigning specific roles and responsibilities to each family member encourages teamwork and accountability, promoting a sense of ownership.

2. **Flexibility in Roles**: Family leaders should remain open to shifting responsibilities as circumstances change, allowing members to step into leadership roles as needed.

Leading by Example

1. **Modeling Desired Behaviors**: Family leaders should exemplify the values and behaviors they wish to instill, such as accountability, kindness, and respect.

2. **Encouraging Independence**: Allowing family members to make choices and learn from their mistakes fosters individual growth while reinforcing that everyone has a role in leadership.

Learning from Leadership Case Studies in Family Dynamics

Successful Leadership Case Study: The Miller Family

The Miller family provides a prime example of effective family leadership:

1. **Establishment of Family Rituals**: The Millers prioritize weekly family game nights, fostering a strong sense of connection and belonging among members.

2. **Open Communication**: Regular family meetings allow everyone to share their perspectives, discuss challenges, and celebrate accomplishments, ensuring everyone's voice is heard.

3. **Conflict Resolution**: When disagreements arise, the Millers employ "I" statements and focus on understanding each other's feelings, leading to healthier resolution practices.

This commitment to communication and connection enriches their family dynamic, creating a supportive environment where each member can thrive.

Lessons from Unsuccessful Leadership: The Johnson Family

The Johnson family illustrates the challenges that can arise from ineffective leadership:

1. **Neglecting Communication**: A lack of communication led to misunderstandings and escalating tensions, which ultimately resulted in the family's fragmentation.

2. **Avoiding Conflict**: Family members often avoided confronting disagreements, leading to unresolved issues that later erupted into larger conflicts.

3. **Inequitable Division of Responsibilities**: An unbalanced distribution of household responsibilities created resentment and feelings of inequity among family members.

These lessons highlight the need for structured communication, conflict resolution, and equitable participation within family dynamics.

Conclusion

Leadership in family dynamics is an essential aspect of fostering healthy relationships, personal growth, and collective well-being. Effective family leaders instill values, nurture open communication, resolve conflicts, and create an environment where every member can flourish. By employing strategies that promote empathy, teamwork, and adaptability, families can navigate the complexities of life while strengthening their bonds.

As we move to the next chapter, we will explore the intersection of leadership across diverse sectors, emphasizing how lessons from family dynamics, social justice, and environmentalism can inform and enrich leaders in various organizational contexts. Understanding these connections will reveal the potential for interdisciplinary collaboration in tackling society's most pressing challenges, ultimately contributing to a more equitable and sustainable world.

Chapter 12: Leadership in Personal Growth

Introduction

Leadership in personal growth is a transformative process that empowers individuals to take control of their lives, set meaningful goals, and cultivate the skills necessary for self-improvement. Whether through formal programs of self-development or informal methods such as reflection and mentorship, the journey of personal growth is deeply intertwined with leadership principles. This chapter delves into the significance of leadership in personal growth, the characteristics of effective personal leaders, the challenges individuals may face, and actionable strategies to foster personal development.

The Role of Personal Leadership

Defining Leadership in Personal Growth

Leadership in personal growth refers to the ability to guide oneself toward self-discovery, self-improvement, and fulfillment. It encompasses the capacity to reflect on one's values, beliefs, and goals while taking proactive steps toward achieving them. Personal leadership involves being accountable to oneself, fostering resilience in the face of challenges, and nurturing a growth mindset.

Key Responsibilities of Personal Leaders

1. **Self-Reflection**: Personal leaders engage in continuous self-reflection to understand their motivations, strengths, and areas for improvement, laying the groundwork for effective goal-setting.

2. **Goal Setting and Planning**: Establishing clear, achievable goals is essential for personal growth, allowing individuals to articulate their vision for the future and create actionable plans.

3. **Resilience Building**: Embracing challenges and setbacks as opportunities for growth is a hallmark of personal leadership. Effective leaders cultivate resilience, enabling them to overcome obstacles.

4. **Seeking Feedback**: Personal leaders are open to constructive feedback, recognizing the importance of external perspectives in their growth journey.

5. **Nurturing Relationships**: Building and maintaining supportive relationships with mentors, peers, and communities is vital for personal growth. Networking and collaboration often lead to new opportunities and insights.

Essential Qualities of Effective Personal Leaders

1. **Self-Awareness**: Understanding one's emotions, strengths, weaknesses, and values is critical for making informed decisions and setting realistic goals.

2. **Vision and Motivation**: Effective personal leaders possess a clear vision for their future and stay motivated to pursue their aspirations, even when faced with obstacles.

3. **Accountability**: Personal leaders hold themselves accountable for their actions, choices, and outcomes, ensuring they remain committed to their goals.

4. **Adaptability**: The ability to adapt to changing circumstances and new information is essential for personal growth. Flexible leaders can pivot when necessary while remaining focused on their overarching objectives.

5. **Emotional Intelligence**: Recognizing and managing one's emotions, as well as empathizing with the emotions of others, aids leaders in fostering meaningful relationships and effectively navigating challenges.

Challenges Facing Personal Leaders

Overcoming Limiting Beliefs

Many individuals harbor limiting beliefs that hinder their personal growth.

1. **Fear of Failure**: Fear can prevent individuals from taking risks or pursuing new opportunities, holding them back from realizing their potential.

2. **Negative Self-Talk**: Internalized criticism and self-doubt can weaken motivation and undermine confidence in one's abilities.

Navigating Life Transitions

Life transitions, such as career changes, relationship shifts, or personal setbacks, can disrupt personal growth and development.

1. **Coping with Uncertainty**: Navigating change often involves uncertainty, making it challenging for individuals to maintain focus on their goals.

2. **Adapting to New Roles**: Transitioning into new professional or personal roles may require individuals to reassess their identity and redefine their goals.

Balancing Responsibilities

Personal leaders often juggle multiple responsibilities, which can lead to stress and burnout.

1. **Time Management**: Finding time for self-reflection, goal-setting, and personal development can be challenging amidst the demands of work, family, and other commitments.

2. **Prioritization**: Striking a balance between personal growth and other responsibilities requires effective prioritization, which can be difficult to navigate.

Strategies for Effective Personal Leadership

Engaging in Self-Reflection

1. **Journaling**: Maintaining a journal allows individuals to articulate their thoughts, feelings, and experiences, fostering greater self-awareness and clarity of purpose.

2. **Mindfulness Practices**: Engaging in mindfulness techniques such as meditation

can help individuals become more attuned to their thoughts and emotions, encouraging reflection and insight.

Setting Clear Goals

1. **SMART Goals**: Establishing Specific, Measurable, Achievable, Relevant, and Time-bound goals enables personal leaders to create tangible objectives and develop actionable plans.

2. **Vision Boards**: Creating visual representations of goals can serve as a daily reminder of aspirations and help maintain focus and motivation.

Cultivating Resilience

1. **Embracing Challenges**: Viewing obstacles as opportunities for growth encourages individuals to step outside their comfort zones and develop resilience.

2. **Developing a Growth Mindset**: Fostering a belief that abilities and intelligence can be developed through dedication and hard work allows individuals to approach challenges with a constructive mindset.

Seeking Feedback and Support

1. **Mentorship**: Establishing relationships with mentors who offer guidance, support, and constructive feedback can significantly enhance personal growth.

2. **Peer Support Groups**: Engaging in community or peer support groups provides opportunities for sharing experiences, networking, and gaining new insights.

Prioritizing Self-Care

1. **Establishing Routines**: Creating daily or weekly routines that incorporate time for self-care activities—such as exercise, relaxation, or hobbies—helps individuals maintain balance and well-being.

2. **Regular Check-Ins**: Periodically assessing progress toward personal goals and making adjustments as needed ensures that individuals remain on track and focused.

Learning from Leadership Case Studies in Personal Growth

Successful Leadership Case Study: Angela's Journey

Angela is a successful professional who transformed her life through personal leadership:

1. **Rediscovery of Purpose**: After feeling unfulfilled in her corporate role, Angela engaged in extensive self-reflection and journaling, which helped her clarify her passions and career goals.

2. **Setting SMART Goals**: She articulated specific goals related to her career transition and developed a clear action plan to pursue opportunities in a field she was passionate about.

3. **Building Resilience**: Angela embraced setbacks—such as job rejections—as learning opportunities, allowing her to adapt her approach and ultimately achieve her dream position.

Angela's story exemplifies the power of self-reflection, resilience, and goal-setting in achieving personal growth.

Lessons from Unsuccessful Leadership: Eric's Challenge

Eric's journey illustrates the pitfalls of ineffective personal leadership:

1. **Fear of Failure**: Eric was paralyzed by a fear of failure, which kept him from pursuing further education or career development opportunities.

2. **Lack of Clarity**: Without clear goals or direction, Eric felt lost and unmotivated, leading to stagnation in both his personal and professional life.

3. **Neglecting Self-Care**: Overwhelmed by responsibilities, Eric neglected his physical and mental well-being, resulting in burnout and decreased motivation.

Eric's experience highlights the importance of setting clear goals, overcoming fears, and prioritizing self-care in the pursuit of personal growth.

Conclusion

Leadership in personal growth is a vital journey that empowers individuals to take charge of their lives, set meaningful goals, and cultivate resilience. By engaging in self-reflection, setting clear objectives, seeking feedback, and prioritizing self-care, personal leaders can navigate challenges and foster continuous development. The qualities of effective personal leaders—such as self-awareness, accountability, and emotional intelligence—are essential in shaping a fulfilling and meaningful life.

As we transition to the concluding chapter, we will explore the interconnected nature of leadership across various domains and emphasize the importance of interdisciplinary collaboration. By synthesizing insights from family dynamics, environmentalism, personal growth, and social justice, we will illuminate how holistic leadership practices can foster positive change in individuals and communities, ultimately contributing to a more equitable, sustainable, and compassionate world.

www.ingramcontent.com/pod-product-compliance
Lightning Source LLC
Chambersburg PA
CBHW031425210526
45464CB00005B/2062